Vince

by
J. B. Midgley

*All booklets are published thanks to the
generous support of the members of the
Catholic Truth Society*

CATHOLIC TRUTH SOCIETY
PUBLISHERS TO THE HOLY SEE

Contents

Acknowledgements

The CTS gratefully acknowledges recourse to the following sources: *Vincent de Paul*, Dr Peter Collet, Nancy, 1748. *Butler's Lives of the Saints*, Ed. M.Walsh, Burns and Oates, 1981. *Encyclopaedia of Catholicism*, Harper and Collins, New York, 1995. *History of Christianity*, O. Chadwick, Weidenfeld and Nicolson, London, 1995. *The Divine Office*, Collins, London, 1974. *The Daily Missal*, Collins, London, 1982. *The Roman Missal*, Burns, Oates & Washbourne, London, 1950. *The Jerusalem Bible*, Darton, Longman & Todd, London, 1974. *The Lives of the Saints*, A. Butler, Virtue & Co., London, 1930. *Dictionary of Saints*, Deformer, Oxford, 1978. *De La Salle, Saint and Spiritual Writer*, W. J. Battersby, Longmans, London, 1950. *De La Salle, Pioneer of Modern Education*, W. J. Battersby, Longmans, London, 1949. *The Papacy*, P. Johnson, Weidenfeld and Nicholson, London, 1997. *Book of Christian Quotations*, T. Castle, Hodder and Stoughton, London, 1982. *Catholic Biographies Volume VII*, Catholic Publishing Society, New York, 1892. *The Heroic Life of St Vincent de Paul*, Henri Lavedan, Sheed & Ward, London, 1929.

ISBN 978 1 86082 503 3

Drinking from the Fount of God's Love

In His kindness, God provides every age with holy men and women to refresh His pilgrim people, and the Holy Spirit breathes an impetus for renewal that is concerned with values, standards, attitudes, religious leadership, and fidelity to the mission Christ has bequeathed to His Church.

The story of Vincent de Paul, founder of the Congregation of the Mission and the Daughters of Charity, and the Patron Saint of Charities, illustrates the essential excellence of the ministerial priesthood on which Christians depend and is at the centre of Catholic life. Though prayer adds nothing to His perfection, God wants those He has created to talk to Him, and bestows the grace to respond to His invitation, often in the company of the Saints whose charity, power and intercession do not diminish with the passing of time. Vincent's eager assistance can be called upon with confidence that he understands present needs.

In the first encyclical of his pontificate, Pope Benedict XVI observed that "the lives of the saints are not limited to their earthly biographies, but continue being and working in God after death. They do not withdraw from

4

men, but rather become truly close to them. Like the Blessed Virgin Mary, they love every generation with a benevolence that results from intimate union with God, through which the soul is totally pervaded by Him, a condition which enables those who have drunk from the fountains of God's love to become, in their turn, a fountain from which 'flow rivers of living water'" (*Deus caritas est*, 2005).

Downham Market,
Lent 2008

Church and Society in the Time of Vincent

Born and raised in final decades of the 16th century, what kind of world awaited the young Vincent? As the Middle Ages drew to a close, there had been growing tension between the papacy and a succession of French rulers who were preoccupied with ensuring the power of their kingdoms. The Protestant Reformation that had complicated matters and events in the years before and after Vincent's birth shed light on the circumstances of his time, his accomplishments, the motivation of his priesthood, and his profound charity.

The effects of Calvinism

John Calvin (1509-1564) was a French lawyer, humanist and Biblical commentator who had once studied for the priesthood before being attracted to Protestantism. He decided that the Church needed restoration to what he believed was her original purity, and went to French speaking Geneva to promote the idea of a Christian state. His treatise *Institutions of the Christian Tradition* expresses the principles of what is termed 'Calvinism'.

Calvin's Geneva community flourished and won many adherents especially in France. Between 1559 and

1561, Calvinist pastors increased the number of Reformed churches there to two thousand that attracted about ten percent of the entire population, a phenomenon that disturbed both the spiritual and secular authorities. The ill-famed Catherine de Medici and her husband Henry II mounted a fierce pursuit of the Protestants who were misappropriating Catholic churches, and this policy incited a rebellion that led to many deaths and a call to arms.

Wars of religion

Vincent, born in 1580, grew up in turbulent times, for when the Reformation first divided Europe into Catholics and Protestants, it did not make any difference to reasons for military action. If it suited them, French Catholics were just as likely to invade Catholic Italy as Protestant Germans and Swiss, and religion was not the initial cause of the civil wars that wracked France from 1562 to 1598. They were more attributable to the sudden death of Henry II in 1559 that left the country without a leader and at the mercy of contending barons.

In 1572, Catherine de Medici's son Charles IX was on the throne of France. On 24th August, the Feast of the Apostle Saint Bartholomew, Admiral Coligny who was a leading Protestant had come to Paris for the wedding of the Protestant King Henry of Navarre to Marguerite, the

Catholic sister of Charles. When an attempt was made to assassinate Coligny, the King panicked and, at the instigation of his mother, ordered the murder of all Protestants in Paris. On this infamous occasion, twenty thousand victims died, including Coligny.

The massacre was the prelude to a succession of fierce religious wars that raged for a quarter of a century until the accession of Henry of Navarre as Henry IV of France. He immediately became a Catholic but showed tolerance to the Huguenots and, in the Edict of Nantes 1598, promised to protect them from oppression. Problems did not disappear overnight, and the general population felt the effects of warfare for a long time. In the seventeenth century, the concessions of civil liberty, freedom of worship, and the provision of fortified cities were eroded, and Louis XIV revoked the Edict on 1685.

Thirty Years War, 1618-1648

At the Peace of Augsburg in 1555, the Catholic German empire accepted the legality of the Protestant faith in Lutheran states and cities. It was, however, an uneasy peace that ended in 1618 when Vincent was thirty-eight. Open hostilities resumed when Bohemian nobles threw two of Emperor Ferdinand's regents out of a window in Prague. With the support of Philip III of Spain, Ferdinand declared war on Frederick V, the Protestant king of

Bohemia, seized Protestant territories, and closed Lutheran churches and schools in Bohemia, Austria and Moravia. The conflict spread across Europe as Lutheran rulers in north Germany and Denmark tried to reclaim lost territories with the assistance of English and Dutch forces. Imperial and Catholic armies defeated them and, in 1629, Ferdinand issued an edict restoring the Catholic properties that Protestants had claimed since 1552.

Council of Trent

Pope Paul III had convened the Council in 1545 to meet the theological challenges of the sixteenth century, but there was little progress until the pontificate of Pope Pius IV. On 3rd December 1563, he confirmed the Council's decrees with the help of his nephew Charles Borromeo who had managed to assemble the two hundred and fifty-five Fathers of the Council for the final session. As a platform for "Counter-Reformation" the Council sought moral reform and an affirmation of traditional Catholic doctrine and devotion. It refuted heresy, clarified the teaching on Original Sin, underlined the permanence of marriage, ended unjust taxation and the sale of Indulgences, condemned clerical concubinage, and brought the bishops under much needed control. It redefined and classified the central beliefs that had been rejected by the Protestant reformers, and have remained characteristic of Catholic expression.

The Council's spiritual and institutional reforms led to refreshed articulation of Catholic theology and related practice that would nourish the Church for four centuries until the Second Vatican Council, following in its footsteps, echoed its authentic teaching about the transmission of Divine Revelation. During the years immediately after the Council of Trent, continuing Catholic Reform was blessed by the labours of many holy men and women.

Many of these great saints had influenced the life of the Church, just at Vincent was growing up.

Saint Charles Borromeo

The Cardinal Archbishop of Milan (1538-1584) has already been mentioned for the telling contributions he made to the Council that included his *Tridentine Catechism* and the initiation of the Confraternity of Christian Doctrine for Children. In 1584 when Pius IV died, Charles was influential in the papal election of Saint Pius V before returning to his diocese from where he led the way in seeing that the Council's directives were implemented. The seminaries he opened raised the level of education, attitudes, and values for those who aspired to the priesthood, and he inspired existing diocesan clergy to lead exemplary lives, often in community, and emulate his abiding concern for the poor.

Saint Theresa of Avila

The Patron of Spain, Theresa (1511-1582), was instrumental in the regeneration of the Carmelite Orders, and founded many convents and friaries that were faithful to the Primitive Rule centred on the worship of God. She also demonstrated how growth in the Mystical Life is the spiritual development that emanates from a love for Our Lord that overflows into love for one's neighbour. People from all walks of life and from every religious affiliation appreciate Theresa's writings and, in 1970, Pope Paul VI declared her a Doctor of the Church. She is first woman to be so honoured.

Saint John of the Cross

The Spanish mystic, poet, and theologian (1542-1591) who was Theresa's great helper in achieving Carmelite reform, is renowned for his treatise *The Dark Night of the Soul* that symbolises the mystical tradition that recalls how Moses after hearing the Ten Commandments on Mount Sinai "approached the dark cloud where God was." 'Darkness', is therefore understood as the meeting with Divine incomprehensibility, the contemplation of human limitations, the shedding of attachments, and the transition from meditation to the gift of contemplation. John saw the journey to God taking place at night, a pilgrimage of faith and trust until a dawn arrival at the mystery of God. He is also a Doctor of the Church.

Saint Philip Neri

Philip (1515-1595) founded the Congregation of the Oratory, an association of priests whose aim is to promote holiness of clerical life, and foster effective preaching. A man of prayer and boundless generosity, he also established a confraternity to assist pilgrims and care for the sick, and was regarded as a living saint by his contemporaries.

Saint Francis de Sales

Francis (1567-1622), the son of a noble family, was born in Savoy in 1567. He studied theology and law at the university of Padua, became a priest, and was consecrated Bishop of Geneva in 1602 when he was only thirty-five. He is remembered for the spiritual direction and support he gave to both clergy and laity through conversations, sermons, letters and treatises, and for his friendship with Vincent de Paul. His writings that include his famous *Introduction to the Devout Life* reveal his thorough understanding of the Church's spiritual tradition, and his sensitive ability to help everyone understand its relevance in every circumstance. Saint Francis was declared a Doctor of the Church by Pope Pius IX in 1877. This is something of the world into which Vincent was born.

Formative Years

Towards the end of the sixteenth century, Paui was a small village near Dax in southern Gascony not far from the Pyrenees. William of Paui (hence Depaul) and his wife Bertrand of Morass owned a small farm here, and they worked very hard to provide for their family of six children. Vincent was the third to be born and, though there is some difference of opinion about the year, the more convincing is that he came into the world on 24th April, 1580, the Tuesday of Easter Week.

The parents' piety and devotion were influential and, from his earliest years, Vincent showed a remarkable love of prayer. The physical demands of rural life were relentless, and children were expected to lend a hand on the farm, if not as soon as they could walk, at least from the age of five. Vincent was allocated the care of the sheep and cattle, and when the region's fierce winds and rain made it necessary, he took shelter in the hollow trunk of an old oak that he turned into a tiny oratory where he prayed to Our Lord, his favourite saints, and particularly to Our Lady, the Blessed Virgin Mary. Nearby, a small chapel dedicated to her was a popular destination with pilgrims, and he regularly collected wild flowers to decorate the altar in a way he thought she deserved.

His concern for others

Though his own family was hardly affluent, Vincent was sensitive towards those in dire poverty, and gave away any coins that came his way either by saving or gift.

Once, when his father sent him to the mill to grind some corn, he gave a handful of flour to a beggar he met on the way back. It says much about William that he did not chide his son for his generosity, though his mother drew the line when he started to distribute some of his clothes that he considered superfluous. There were already signs that he would serve Christ in the persons of the poor, and his parents who recognised that he was intelligent, quick to learn, kind, and devout, wondered if he might have a vocation to the priesthood. They decided that he should be educated accordingly, and when he was twelve they entrusted him to the care of the Franciscan Recollects who ran a school in Dax. Making no small sacrifice, they managed to find the money for his board and lodging.

Star student

Vincent made excellent progress, and when he was sixteen his abilities were noticed by Monsieur de

Commet, a well known lawyer in the area. He had heard
the Franciscan Fathers warmly praising their star pupil
who had just completed his preliminary studies, and
chose him to be his children's tutor. This enabled Vincent
to continue his studies and ease his parents' financial
burden. Two years later, he enrolled in the university of
Toulouse to read Theology in preparation for his
ordination to the priesthood and received the tonsure, the
rite of initiation into the clerical state that involves
shaving some hair from crown of the head. When his
father sold off part of his herd of cattle, he sent Vincent
some money that enabled him to visit the university of
Saragossa. Perhaps it was a sign of the times, but he was
soon disenchanted by the concentration on speculative
arguments about grace at the expense of orthodox
divinity, and was glad to return to Toulouse.

Ordination

In 1600, Vincent was ordained priest at the early age of
twenty. He celebrated his first Mass in an isolated chapel
because he did not want any public ceremonial to distract
him from the sublime dignity of the moment that was to
remain with him all his life. When his father died soon
afterwards, he declined his share of a small inheritance
and chose to support himself by becoming schoolmaster
to the sons and daughters of the neighbourhood gentry.

He continued with his university studies until he graduated in Divinity and, as was customary, delivered public lectures in Theology. These won such acclaim that he was offered a parish with income attached but, when a fellow priest laid claim, he withdrew from the contest to avoid distasteful litigation. He grew in reputation as an able and orthodox theologian who was well versed in the Scriptures, the writings of the Fathers and the lives of the Saints, and blessed with all the virtues that characterise a zealous minister of the altar. He had not yet reached the heroic self-denial and burning charity of the saint who experiences the tribulations through which the Holy Spirit prepares souls for the works of Grace in the Mystery of the Cross, but trials and setbacks were soon to lay the foundation of the higher virtue that he would attain.

Captivity and slavery

In 1605, Vincent went to Marseilles to settle the affairs of a friend who had recently died there. The return journey involved taking ship to Narbonne across the northern Mediterranean, and then overland to Toulouse but, as the vessel sailed through the Gulf of Lions, it was attacked by Turkish pirates. The passengers and crew resisted bravely but some were killed, and the rest sustained injury, including Vincent who was badly wounded by an arrow.

The survivors were clapped in irons and taken to Tunis to be sold as slaves.

The treatment and conditions they had to endure on the lengthy voyage were horrendous and had a lasting impact on Vincent's health. He described their eventual arrival at port where "the slave merchants came to see who could eat heartily and who could not, and to examine if our wounds were mortal. That done, they took us to the great Square where the merchants inspected us as if they were buying a horse, making us open our mouths to see our teeth, probing our wounds, forcing us to show our paces, to trot, run, lift weights to show strength, and a thousand other brutalities."

Vincent was bought by a fisherman but, since he showed little aptitude for the marine tasks involved and was prone to chronic sea sickness, the relationship was not a success and he was sold on to an apothecary. The new master was kind and grew very fond of his new slave whom he wanted to train as his successor when he retired. Vincent had other ideas, but served him conscientiously until his death in 1606 when, as part of the estate, he was inherited by the apothecary's nephew who quickly sold him to a lapsed Christian from Nice in Savoy who had a small farm.

Compassion for the suffering

His new owner was involved in an eccentric domestic
arrangement involving three wives at the same time. One
of these was so impressed by Vincent's behaviour, his
uncomplaining response to the harsh demands of labour,
and obviously vibrant belief, that she took her husband to
task for abandoning such a precious faith. She insisted
that her husband should engineer the slave's return to his
own country. The heart of the Savoyard was touched; he
resolved to repent and, at the first opportunity, set off
with Vincent across the Mediterranean in a dangerously
small boat. They eventually landed near Marseilles in
June 1607, and made their way to Avignon where the
wandering sheep was received back to the Church's fold
by the Papal Legate.

When the two expressed a wish to make a pilgrimage
to Rome, the Legate facilitated the visit and introduced
Vincent in the Papal Court. There he came to the
attention of the French Ambassador who was grateful
for his thoughtful advice, and entrusted him with
communications to the court of Henry IV. When
Vincent finally returned to France, he was appointed
chaplain to Queen Margaret of Valois, and a
comfortable, privileged career seemed to beckon.
However, the slavery experience had deeply affected
him and awakened a compassion for all who suffered

hardship or were exposed to mortal danger. During the period in Rome, the example of the Apostles and Martyrs had inspired him to pray for the grace to emulate their heroic virtues, and another experience was about to further his spiritual development.

Renouncement of self

Vincent declined the ecclesiastical advancement and advantages the Crown was able to offer, including the revenues of an abbey, and decided to lodge in an unfashionable quarter of Paris where he shared rooms with a magistrate from his home region. He became very involved in visiting a local hospital and doing all he could to help the sick and those who cared for them. Unfortunately, when the magistrate discovered that some money was missing from his room, he accused Vincent of the theft and defamed him in public. Vincent's only response was to say, "God knows the truth," and it was some time before his name was cleared, when the real culprit was caught stealing again and confessed to the earlier offence. Years later, in spiritual conference with his priests, he related this story in the third person to illustrate that patience, silence, and resignation, are the fruitful means of sanctifying those who suffer slander and persecution.

A 'Call within a Call'

Influence of Pierre de Berulle

In the course of his hospital visits, Vincent met and immediately forged a lasting friendship with Father Pierre de Berulle (1575-1629), who played a major role in the Catholic revival of the seventeenth century. He is honoured as the founder of the distinctive French School of Spirituality that benefited from Vincent's own contribution, and remained an exemplary influence in the Church until the twentieth century. Pierre, who was to become a Cardinal, was the most eminent theologian, writer and spiritual director of his day, and had a deep concern for the reform and education of the clergy. The upheavals of the Reformation and the civil wars had left the Church in need of new vigour.

Many of the clergy had abandoned their cassocks and adopted the dress and manners of cavaliers, rather like Aramis in Dumas' story of the *The Three Musketeers*. Freethinking was popular, and Church teaching either ignored or opposed. Inspired by the pioneering work of Saint Philip Neri, Pierre founded the French Congregation of the Oratory in 1611, a body of priests living in community and seriously prepared to exercise their sacred and essential ministry. His example was followed by Father Adrian Bourdoise who opened the Seminary of Saint-Nicholas-du-Chardonnet a year later, by Vincent himself who began to educate clergy in 1628 and by Jean Jaques Olier at the renowned Saint Sulpice in 1642, about which more will be said later.

Father Pierre did much to restore the spirit of religion that leads to the worship of God with due reverence and adoration. He taught that through Baptism the Christian commits himself to adore the divine perfections, the will and judgement of God, and the mysteries of His Son. "This is what we must do all our life because it is the first thing that God commands us and, as Our Lord says, it contains all the law. Our love for God should be so great that we should love nothing but Him and for Him...Christians unite this relationship with God to the mysteries of Jesus that are ever present in their effect and will never pass away."

This theme was later developed by Saint John Eudes (1601-1680), who wrote, "We must use our days and years in cooperating with Jesus in the divine task of completing His mysteries in us." Saint John Baptist de La Salle (1651-1719), likewise recommended to his followers the practice of uniting themselves, their prayers, work, even their relaxation, and their assistance at Holy Mass to "the merits and dispositions of Jesus Christ, the Victim immolated for the glory of the Father."

First spiritual struggles

Vincent was understandably reluctant to repeat the unhappy experience of shared lodgings, and was delighted when Pierre offered him a room in the community house of the Congregation of the French Oratory then in its infancy. It proved a providential blessing to have the supportive presence of others because another traumatic test awaited him. A brother priest, though not of the community, had earned a fine reputation as a theologian who spoke out fearlessly against heresy. Queen Margaret, who liked to surround herself with intellectuals of integrity, appointed him to a position in court that she believed would benefit from his presence. However, the idle life severely depressed the priest and caused him mental anguish. His health deteriorated, and a crisis of faith made him unable to pray and recite the Divine Office. He was on the verge of suicide when Vincent met him, took pity on him, and asked God to transfer the man's burdens to himself.

As quickly as faith and peace of mind returned to the sufferer, it ebbed away from Vincent, but he employed saintly tactics to deal with temptation and did the exact opposite of what the Devil suggested. In the midst of

confusion he remembered the Church's teaching that we
have to make an effort in the spiritual battle, and that prayer
is our determined response to the gift of grace. He prayed,
hoped, did penance, behaved as if doubt did not exist, and
wrote a profession of faith that disclaimed any thoughts of
disbelief. He still had to struggle valiantly for a long time,
always praying with the Psalmist, "Give me again the joy of
your help; with a spirit of fervour sustain me…O Lord open
my lips and my mouth shall declare your praise" (*Ps 50*).

Call to 'feed the hungry and clothe the naked'

One day, after a storm of doubt more violent than ever, he
solemnly resolved to follow Our Lord's example and accept
His divine legacy to feed the hungry, clothe the naked,
comfort the fragile, befriend the marginalised, welcome the
stranger, care for the sick, visit the imprisoned, reconcile
antagonists, and love His brothers and sisters as He loves
them. The clouds lifted, never again to come between him
and a clear-sighted faith and, in 1748, his biographer Pierre
Collet of Nancy was able to write "he was imbued to a
remarkable degree with the common sense that is perhaps
more rare than genius, for it requires a collection and balance
of attitudes: clear sightedness to comprehend an idea, breadth
of vision to embrace all implications, discernment to
recognise circumstances and anticipate consequences, and
judgement to preside over implementation."

Parish priest of Clichy

In 1612, Father Pierre, who was now Vincent's spiritual director, suggested that he serve the parishioners as parish priest in Clichy, a village outside Paris. He had scarcely left the Court when he was deeply saddened by the assassination of Henry IV whom he regarded as a great king. Despite his faults, he loved him dearly and afterwards would say of him, "By becoming a child of the Church, he made himself the father of France." He threw himself wholeheartedly into the work of the parish, and showed such amazing zeal that people loved him as soon as they met him. He took an individual interest in them, consoling, guiding and, as far as the duties of ministry allowed, being their special friend without showing favouritism. He coaxed with gentle affability and depicted virtue and sacrifice in such vibrant colours that they became desirable. He shepherded the lukewarm to fervent observance, gave hope to the afflicted, healed those who thought themselves lost, and guided back to religious duties those who had previously despised them.

He rebuilt the dilapidated church and embellished the interior to the extent that his flock took pleasure and pride upon entering for a service or to make a visit to the Blessed Sacrament. Money for the costs seemed to materialise miraculously without making demands on the parishioners. Vincent was so happy at Clichy that he said, "the Pope is not as happy as I am." But Father Pierre had another task for him that, despite the pain of departure after only six months, he accepted as the will of God. All the villagers, whether his parishioners or not, were grief stricken.

Chaplain to the Gondi family

The reason for Vincent's departure was that Father Pierre had asked him to undertake the education of Peter and Henry, two of the sons of Emmanuel and Frances Gondi, Count and Countess of Joigny. The position included being chaplain to the illustrious household, and the innumerable retainers, workers, tenants, and residents on the Gondi's huge estates that were akin to a sizeable realm. It was a far-flung 'parish', but Pierre knew what an influential apostolate it offered. Vincent resolutely embarked on teaching the two boys the essence of nobility, obedience since they were destined to command, their duty to God, the just use of wealth since the poor are always with us, and preparation for the important positions in Church and State for which they were born.

Countess Frances was a splendid mother, devout yet practical. She valued Vincent's teaching skills, wisdom, and holiness, and chose him as her life-long spiritual director and confessor. When she heard that he had helped a dying man to make a general confession and meet his death peacefully, she asked him to recommend the salutary comfort and spiritual benefits of general confession to all her dependants. On 25th January 1617, the feast of the Conversion of Saint Paul, he preached a sermon on this subject, and the response was so great that he had to enlist the assistance of the Jesuits at Amiens to serve the crowd of penitents.

When he was not devoting himself to his pupils, the care of souls, and wide-ranging works of charity with Frances' support, Vincent avoided the pomp and circumstance of the Gondi court, and turned his room into a monastic cell. "This simplicity," he said, "was of great service because I saw only God in all the people with who whom I dealt, and brought myself to do nothing in their sight that I would not have done in the presence of Our Lord, had I ever had the honour to talk to Him during His mortal life." In the course of time, Peter became Duke of Retz but Henry died tragically young in a riding accident. A third younger son is remembered as Cardinal de Retz, but not with universal admiration.

Ministering to galley crews

As Marshall of the French Galleys, Emmanuel Gondi was responsible for the convicts and outcasts of society who were enslaved to provide the rowing power for fighting ships. They were treated abominably and, in desperation, they railed against God as the cause of all their woe. Only the patience and heroic charity of a saint could give them any possible consolation. Vincent assumed the role of Chaplain in Chief to the French fleet, and this gave him the opportunity and influence to make their conditions more humane. He built a hospital to care for those who were worn out from their labours and, on one occasion, he substituted for one of the prisoners so that he could visit his wife and children about whom he was desperately worried. He made light of the ulcers that the shackles caused and would discomfort him for the rest of his life, and proceeded to expand his chaplaincy function by conducting missions to convicts in Bordeaux.

Gathering his first companions

Father Pierre next directed Vincent to attend to the needs of the rural communities of Bresse whose parishes were failing. The Gondi family, especially Frances, were so devastated by even a temporary absence that he left quietly so as not to cause further grief. From his own experience, pastoral zeal, and astute assessment of diocesan clergy, Vincent had already identified the need for a group of secular priests who would live in community and support one another to the best possible advantage in the care of souls. He invited five like-minded priests to join him in a flexible, broad apostolate, and they formed a small community in the parish of Chatillon-des-Dombes. It was a dismal place that still bore the scars of the religious conflict, with houses abandoned or appropriated by vagabonds, and a dispirited community. There had been no permanent parish priest for over a century and the faithful had been served only by visiting clergy who did little more than collect the attached revenues.

Tending the lost sheep

In less than a year, Vincent and his little group transformed a dreadful situation first by bringing the neighbouring clergy and faithful of the region to a more positive frame of mind, and through their own personal routine of rising at dawn, praying the Divine Office, celebrating Mass every day, visiting everyone without distinction whether Catholic or Protestant, healthy or sick, and undertaking property maintenance that included the restoration of the neglected church in Chatillon. Vincent's biographer, Henri Lavedan wrote, "When he was not working, he was in the church where he welcomed every person who came with a smile. He did not know the meaning of impatience and, though he accepted all the burdens they came to unload on him, he was never tired out by them. Other people's burdens strengthened him but they made his back grow rounder day by day like a miller's bent beneath sacks of the finest flour, like a carrier's – a Carrier of the Cross." Conversions and returns to the Faith came in blessed abundance, the churches filled for Mass and other devotions, the people became happy and optimistic, and the miracle of Clichy had been repeated.

Conversions of heart

Some astonishing changes of heart are worth mentioning as an example of Vincent's God-given charisma. The Count de Rougemont was a local aristocrat and landowner who had a justifiable reputation as a debauched, violent, irascible, and irreligious maniac preoccupied with duelling. He was intrigued by the glowing reports of Vincent's virtues and eloquence, and wanted to judge for himself. When he heard Vincent preach, he was so moved that he declared himself a criminal worthy of punishment and in need of atonement. He made a general confession to Vincent, sold the Rougemont estate, divided the proceeds among the poor and religious houses, and broke his sword, a painful sacrifice for a 'gentleman'. Two fashionable ladies in the area, who were living frivolous, scandalous lives, had an immediate change of heart when they met Vincent. They abandoned their affairs wishing only to love God, became his enthusiastic and energetic helpers, and devoted the rest of their lives to the service of the poor.

Vincent's Apostolate is Born

The Congregation of the Mission

When Countess Frances saw the success of the collaborative mission to Bresse, she was determined that all her subjects living on the Gondi's far-flung estates should benefit from similar ministry. She gave practical help with funding and her brother John, who was Archbishop of Paris, gave Vincent's nascent community the College of Les Bons Enfants where they settled in 1625.

For the time being, Vincent remained at the Gondi court but when Frances died shortly afterwards, he went to live with his priests, and drew up a Constitution that was approved by Pope Urban VIII in 1632, and King Louis XIII gave letters patent to the "Congregation of the Mission". The Rule included the prescription of an hour's meditation every morning, self-examination of conduct three times a day, the observance of silence except during the hours designated for conversation, and an annual retreat of eight days. The Congregation of secular priests live in community and take simple vows of poverty, chastity, obedience and stability, and refrain from ecclesiastical promotion. Its aims are the sanctification of members, taking the Gospel to the poor especially in rural areas and remote townships, administering parishes, working to convert sinners, conducting missions at home and abroad, educating the clergy and candidates for the priesthood in their own and diocesan seminaries, and promoting Catholic education. Every mission began with spending a month in the particular place, teaching catechism, preaching, hearing confessions, reconciling differences, and engaging in works of charity.

Growing in numbers

In 1633, the Canons Regular of Saint Victor donated the church and priory of Saint Lazare in Paris to the new and growing congregation. According to an eleventh century legend, Lazarus of Bethany, whom Our Lord had raised from the dead, and his sisters Martha and Mary were put to sea in a boat without rudder or oars by hostile Jews. They landed in south eastern Gaul and successfully preached the Gospel in the Marseilles area where Lazarus eventually became Bishop before being martyred during the persecution of Domitian, 81-96 AD. The priory now became the Congregation's headquarters in France where they were known as "Lazarists", though many now refer to them affectionately as the "Vincentians". The buildings and site of Saint-Lazare were so extensive they had once accommodated a hospital. Such facilities and the revenues that were historically attached to the priory "enabled good works to pour from here as from an inexhaustible spring." Vincent worked ceaselessly, at the same time treating himself severely. He wore a hair shirt, scourged himself, fasted, and spent long hours in prayer kneeling on a usually cold floor. With Saint Augustine, he knew that "Our chief work is the praise of God and that the goal of our journey to the Father's house is to worship Him in His glory and beauty."

Work of the Congregation expands

The desperate need of the many beggars who roamed the streets of Paris made some violent and a threat to others. Vincent managed to acquire the redundant buildings of a manufacturing plant, and converted these into a place where they could be sheltered and given some decent order of life. He persuaded the Government to prohibit begging and undertake financial responsibility for the development and maintenance of the project he had initiated, and the priests of the Congregation attended to the spiritual care of four thousand or so souls who were accommodated. He urged all his helpers and followers to look on the poor as their masters who, he admitted, "could be insensitive and demanding, dirty, ugly, unjust, and foul mouthed. The harder they are to serve, the more you will have to love them." In the years to come he would say, "I do not notice the rough exterior, coarseness, or even the foolishness of the poor. I look at the other side of the medal and see nothing but the Son of God, poor by His own choice, a folly to the Gentiles, a scandal to the Jews." He understood perfectly what Our Lord had intended to convey in His parable about the Lost Sheep, and explained to others that "there is no human being who is beyond redemption, no one who is not loved deeply, personally, and eternally by God the Father who does not want any one to be lost."

His love for the poor and determination to serve them did not blind him to human foibles, and he believed that relief should be associated with transformation of life. He told one shiftless young man who was queuing for free bread that, "Providence looks after the birds, but at least they do something." Noticing the strapping physique of another, he pointed out that his obviously muscular arm was strong enough to use a spade. His charitable eye missed nothing and, throughout his life, he combined his devotion to the poor and oppressed with his apostolate to the wealthy and fashionable. He was concerned, for example, about the evil of duelling which, despite being illegal, was still the frequent method of settling "matters of honour". He therefore organised an association of men who made a solemn promise never to make or accept a challenge, and many courtiers and army officers signed the commitment.

Responding to Cromwell's Irish invasion

After the execution of Charles I of England in 1640, and Ireland's declaration of support for his son, Oliver Cromwell went there and crushed such rebellion with ferocity. Vincent's heart went out to the suffering people, and he sent them clothes, money, and five intrepid Vincentians who had volunteered to minister to the needs of the besieged in Limerick and Cashel. Encouraged by Vincent's frequent messages, the priests' devotion was constant in the face of great danger from the occupying forces and the plague that had broken out, and the people of Ireland gratefully remember their heroism to this day.

After Cromwell's invasion, many Catholics fled to join the army in France still embroiled in the Thirty Years War. When two Irish Regiments suffered great losses, Vincent asked an Irish member of the Congregation to help families and the wounded, and he himself set about raising money so that those left homeless could be housed and fed. In response to famine and devastation brought by the so-called wars of religion, Vincent and his brother priests lived on bare necessities so that they could send money saved to alleviate the suffering of the people. So persuasively did he enlist the help of the Court and all who were in a position to contribute, that he raised funds sufficient to support twenty-three towns through the worst times, always with an infectious confidence that God would bless and multiply human efforts.

Missions overseas

Other missions and charitable endeavours away from home included Tunis that was the scene of Vincent's early captivity, Madagascar, and Corsica.

Vincent lived to see twenty-five houses of his Congregation established in France, Italy, and the wider Europe. Everywhere, the Vincentians followed the new meaning their Founder had given to the parish as a centre for the spiritual life, and also for the charitable and communal activities of its members. In this approach, he anticipated the revitalisation envisaged by the Second Vatican Council, 1965, by three centuries.

Expansion continued throughout the world, and the Fathers of the Congregation were immediately and remarkably effective in America where they soon opened parishes, schools and later universities, including St John's on Long Island, Nicaragua in New York, and De Paul in Chicago.

Daughters of Charity

Saint Francis of Assisi had nourished the spiritual life of the Church by teaching his Friars and Sisters to give their possessions to the poor, to share their poverty and, as mendicant beggars, depend on the charity of others to stay alive. Vincent, on the other hand, gathered men and women together to provide food and shelter for the needy, care for the sick, and see the crucified Christ in the faces of the homeless and marginalised.

Christ in the poor

He recognised the truth that the Incarnation dignified and sanctified every human being that God has made in His own image, and that what is done for the least of His brothers and sisters is done for Christ who is God. Because he found the poor in Christ and Christ in the poor he maintained, "If you are in the chapel saying your prayers, and someone who needs you is at the door, you must leave God to attend to God."

He assembled groups of wealthy, devout ladies whom he organised to help the poor and sick. They were whole-hearted in raising and administering funds, and

36

dealing with correspondence, but their domestic responsibilities limited the time they could devote to charitable work. Furthermore, their privileged background did not really equip them for nursing the poor in their own homes, the physical demands of hospital care, supporting neglected children, or communicating effectively with those husbands and fathers who could be uncouth to say the least. The maidservants occasionally sent as their substitutes, gave only grudging assistance, and Vincent decided that, if the work was to grow, something more permanent than voluntary involvement was needed, especially from women who were more familiar with the social background of the sufferers.

Louise de Marillac

In the course of his tireless missions, Vincent had met young women of exemplary life and high ideals, who felt called to the Religious Life, not necessarily in convent enclosure, but whose poverty and lack of dowry made entry difficult. When some of these told him they wanted to devote themselves to the arduous task of nursing the sick, Providence set to work.

Louise de Marillac (1591-1660), came from an aristocratic family, was married and had one son. After her husband's death in 1625 she decided to give herself to the service of God and, by happy chance, met Vincent who agreed to her request to be her spiritual counsellor. He quickly came to appreciate her courage, endurance and selflessness. It was not long after he had been given the Saint-Lazare premises that he asked her if she would train the willing girls and widows of modest background to serve the sick and the poor. She started immediately with four candidates at her Paris home in the Rue des Fosses-Saint-Victor, and their example was soon attracting many others.

The scope of charity was breathtaking as Vincent pursued the relief of others in their spiritual and corporal needs. He established confraternities like the Dames of the Cross to educate young girls, work in hospitals, and care for children who were orphaned, ill-treated, or exploited. He directed the foundation of hospitals, opened a home for elderly men, and the hospital for the galley slaves in Mareilles where the members of his Congregation were now chaplains. Somehow, the necessary money always appeared, and his magnetism never failed to attract the wealthy who were willing to collect funds and give practical help in his innumerable charitable enterprises that financed missions to Scotland and Poland as well as Ireland, and provided shelter, clothing and sustenance for those still suffering from the aftermath of religious conflict.

New Order born

At first, Vincent had not envisaged a religious order but more a gathering of Christian women wanting to serve the sick and the poor. He told the first voluntary group, "Your convent will be the house of the sick, your chapel the parish church, your cloister the city streets or the hospital wards, your enclosure obedience, your grill the fear of God, your veil modesty." When it became evident, however, that they wanted to combine this work with a vocation to the Religious Life, he drew up a Rule appropriate to their unique calling. Religious Life was usually either monastic and conventual for monks and nuns who lived according to the Rule of, say, Saint Benedict or Saint Basil, or the Rule of Saint Augustine adopted by the Canons and Canonesses Regular. The new community marked a departure from the tradition of the cloistered life by spending most of their time outside the convent, and making private vows annually.

Vincent entrusted his new order, the Daughters of Charity, to the spiritual care of the Congregation of the Mission, and appointed Louise to be the first Mother Superior. Their impact was immediate as they took charge of the Hotel Dieu hospital in Paris, nursed those who had been struck down by the plague in the city, and reorganised a failing hospital in Angers. Then, they undertook the training necessary to conduct primary schools for the education of impoverished children in rural districts.

In Paris, there were many children orphaned by the regular waves of crime, and infants were left in church doorways by widowed mothers unable to cope. There was an official home for foundlings, but it was inadequately funded, and staffed by questionable personnel who gave or sold the inmates to unsuitable adoptive "parents". When Vincent and Louise visited the establishment they were horrified by the conditions, and it seemed as if the civil strife had numbed a sense of morality. As a first step in reversing a deplorable situation, they took eight of the hapless innocents into the Sisters' care. Vincent provided money from the revenues of the Saint-Lazare priory, used his influence to persuade the State to make a generous donation and, in due course, to build and endow a satisfactory Foundling Hospital.

Distinctive mission and identity

The Sisters have their foundations all over the world, and have won universal admiration. As with his Congregation, Vincent had always believed that wearing a distinctive religious habit contributes to perseverance and stability, and helps the laity recognise that those who have embraced the Religious Life are separate from the World. Until modification in the twentieth century, the Daughters of Charity were distinguished by their grey habit and large "Cornette" headdress of white linen that was the usual clothing of Breton peasant women. They remain shining lights in charity to which Vincent had brought such effective organisation, and is still seen in today's shelters and soup kitchens for the homeless.

Vincent and Saint Francis de Sales

In 1610, Francis cooperated with Saint Jane Frances de Chantal (1572-1641), to found the Order of the Sisters of the Visitation. In 1619 they were opening one of their convents in Paris when they met Vincent, and there was an immediate meeting of minds. It is a measure of the esteem in which they held him that they entrusted him with the spiritual care of the Sisters. Francis, in particular, became Vincent's great friend and admirer.

Education of the Clergy

By now, the Congregation of the Mission was conducting Retreats for parochial clergy, and Vincent introduced the practice of the "Tuesday Conference" to keep alive "the fire of charity that had been kindled" during these withdrawals for prayer, meditation, spiritual development, and study. The priests who attended them observed some simple but well-defined rules that he offered them in the cause of their own sanctification, and they met regularly to benefit from his guidance on the duties and accomplishment of their vocation. They acquired such a fine reputation that he was often asked by Cardinal Richlieu, Louis XIII's Minister of State, to recommend names when bishoprics fell vacant and, as a result, he was instrumental in the appointment of twenty-three bishops and archbishops.

In 1662, Pope Alexander VII stipulated that in the See of Rome and its six associate dioceses, ordination to the priesthood must first be preceded by a ten day retreat directed by the Fathers of Vincent's Congregation.

Seminary education

One of the Tuesday Conference confraternity was Father Jean Jacques Olier, the parish priest of Saint Sulpice in Paris. He shared Vincent's views about seminary education, and both were conscious of the Council of Trent's decree that every diocese or group of dioceses should have a seminary to prepare well-trained and devoted parochial clergy. They also knew that success was variable and that many students dropped out because they were unsuitable, disappointed, or decided to join a religious order.

In 1641, Father Olier assembled a group of priests who wanted to dedicate themselves to the religious and intellectual formation of candidates for the priesthood. The community lived in a house attached to the church and opened the first seminary of the Society of Saint Sulpice on the premises.

Courses for students to the priesthood

Father Olier wanted to help aspirants to the priesthood to be holy and cultured men who were expert in the knowledge that their incomparable mission required. "Care must be taken, "he wrote, "that there is nothing wanting in the instruction of clerics regarding doctrine and piety. The Society of Saint Sulpice will provide instruction for each one according to his ability in Philosophy, Scholastic and Moral Theology, and Polemics. In the pulpit, the priest must speak for the learned as well as the ignorant, uphold the truths of the Gospel, combat vice, resist the torrent of prevailing opinion, and confound heresy. Unmasking subterfuge and what is false requires a deeper and wider knowledge than that acquired by private study, a knowledge to be tested in the schools and academies." Consequently, his seminarians attended courses at the university of the Sorbonne that was then a stronghold of uncontaminated faith and a bastion against heresy.

Dispute with Jansenism

One of Vincent's contemporaries was Cornelius Jansen (1585-1638), a Flemish theologian, Bishop of Ypres, and dedicated student of Saint Augustine of Hippo. His treatise *Augustinus*, published in 1640 two years after his death, unfortunately carried Augustine's theology too far by advocating a rigorous spirituality that attempted to stifle human nature that was regarded as essentially corrupt. The interpretation of grace and free will was similar to Protestant belief in the sufficiency of grace, and was contrary to Catholic teaching that we must cooperate with God's grace through good works. The followers of Jansen emphasised the irresistible character of grace and so undervalued free will, recommended a severe morality, and were dubious about the chances of salvation for the majority.

One of Vincent's friends, Father John Verger, the Parish Priest of Saint Cyran had been Jansen's fellow student at Louvain University, was attracted to his theories, and even tried to recruit Vincent to the heresy. Vincent was horrified and gently pleaded with him to hold fast to what is of faith, but soon realised that he was encumbered by intellectual pride. When Verger published a work advising abstinence from Holy Communion on the pretext of respect for the Blessed Sacrament, Vincent publicly refuted the fallacy and told the hierarchy that they must ask the Pope for a judgement, otherwise the Church in France would be in conflict. He was relieved when Pope Innocent X condemned Jansenism in 1653, and gently tried to persuade its leading exponents to accept the Papal ruling but with little success. Verger became director of the Convent at Port-Royal that was a centre of Jansenism that attracted a strong following, especially in France where Catholics interpreted the Pope's action as an affront to their independence and integrity. In the ensuing tension, a national movement with theological overtones asserted that Papal authority could be exercised only through a General Council to which its decrees must be subject, but this did not deter Vincent from actively opposing the heresy.

Later Years and Homecoming

Cardinal Armand Richelieu died in 1642, after eighteen years as Louis XIII's First Minister. Vincent had been fearless in opposing his policy of French independence from the See of Peter in Rome, and his alignment with German and Swiss Protestants against the Catholic Hapsburgs during the Thirty Years War. That same year, he attended the King during his final illness and helped him to meet death peacefully and with resignation.

Louis' widow, Queen Anne of Austria, came to rely increasingly on Vincent's wise advice and, as Regent, appointed him to the Council of Conscience of the young Louis XIV and to a permanent commission with responsibility to nominate candidates to fill vacant Bishoprics and other senior positions in the Church. The commission was headed by Cardinal Jules Mazarin who, as well as becoming the new First Minister in 1643, enjoyed a number of ecclesiastical benefices even though he was not in Holy Orders.

Constant in resisting secularism

Vincent failed to convince Anne that she should dispense with the services of Mazarin who was pursuing interests of State at the expense of the Church and the Papacy, but his influence at Court remained powerful during the period of her regency. With courteous and articulate determination, he voiced opposition to policies he considered contrary to the Church's mission and, in the face of secular opposition, was instrumental in the English Benedictine nuns from Ghent opening a convent in Boulogne. Above all, he was the Father and Superior of his Congregation whose members emulated their holy founder's zeal for souls.

Good and faithful servant

In 1658, Vincent had a presentiment that his apostolate was in its final stages. Always the realist, he knew that ceaseless work, fatigue, personal mortification, and the period of captivity in Tunis had weakened a once robust constitution. He gathered together all the beloved members of his Congregation at the Motherhouse of Saint-Lazare and gave each of them a little book of directions that he hoped would help the exact observance of their religious life, and the fulfilment of its responsibilities.

He recommended to his disciples the self-denial, profound humility, and a spirit of prayer permeating all aspects of life's activities through which he had sought to achieve his own degree of perfection. They were well aware that, no matter how busy he was, he made the Sign of the Cross and an act of love whenever the clock struck the hour. They saw that no matter how unpromising the circumstances, he maintained serenity of mind, and was undisturbed by slander, disappointment, and opposition because he bowed to God's will that he glorified in all things, even his own suffering. For then he wrote, "Our highest ambition is to instruct the ignorant, to bring sinners to repentance and to plant the gospel-spirit of charity, humility, meekness, and simplicity in the hearts of all Christians."

Failing health and death

When Vincent reached his eightieth year in 1660, he reluctantly accepted the necessity of getting from place to place by using a horse-drawn carriage that he nicknamed 'my disgrace.' Typically, if he saw anyone in the street suffering from sickness and poverty, and there were many, he would struggle down, help them in, and drive them to the nearest hospital or refuge. He never let failing health impede his devotion to others, nor did he allow thoughts of his own comfort to distract him from putting others first. He was becoming worn out, and in September he contracted an agonising fever that was accompanied by violent and enervating perspiration.

Despite the fact that much needed sleep eluded him, he continued to get up at four o'clock to say his morning

48

prayers that might continue for three hours before he said Mass. After this, he touchingly recited the Prayers for the Dying with his brethren in preparation for his own final hour. When Pope Alexander VII heard of his illness, he immediately dispensed him from the duty of reciting the Divine Office, but his thoughtful message did not arrive in time. On 27th September, Vincent was sitting in his chair because he was too weak to be helped to bed. One of his priests asked him to bless the Congregation and, in reply, he echoed Saint Paul, "He who hath begun a good work will perfect it." With these words, the good and faithful servant sped to the joy of his Lord.

A lasting legacy

Vincent was already a legend revered by clergy, laity, rich, poor, outcasts and convicts, all of whom had experienced the goodness of a man who had no thought of self and was totally consumed by love of God and love of neighbour. All France was saddened at his passing, especially the people of Paris where the renown of his sanctity and his marvellous work for the poor was on everyone's lips. His work, influence, and skills had brought a major change in social consciousness in France that would be to the benefit of Europe and the whole world.

Clergy, and laity from every section of society attended the Requiem Mass and funeral that were without the simplicity Vincent would have preferred, and the citizens thronged to Saint-Lazare in such numbers that city activity was suspended for the entire day. The poor were chosen as his bodyguard and with them came his Congregation of the Mission, the Daughters of Charity, prelates, members of the nobility, and the Papal Nuncio. His heart was enclosed in a silver vase and his body buried, first in front of the high altar in Saint-Lazare's gothic church, and later translated to the crypt where pilgrims came to pray, seek Vincent's intercession, and venerate his relics.

The City of Reims had a poignant reason to mourn his death because while the religious conflicts raged, the money he raised and sent regularly relieved the suffering and fed the poor. A commemoration Mass was celebrated in the Cathedral, and undoubtedly the future Saint, John Baptist de La Salle, was present. The nine year old would have heard of Vincent's splendid achievements and perhaps formed a vision of another fruitful apostolate to be exercised. A benign Providence was arranging that as Vincent's life ended, another champion of the poor was emerging.

Devotion to Saint Vincent de Paul

The early biographers record that during his life, Vincent made accurate predictions of future events, the consequences of lukewarm attitudes, and the foolishness of ignoring God and His commandments. They also state that the many miracles wrought through his intercession increased after his death, especially in France and Italy.

Miracles

One of these benefited Father Bonnet, the rector of the Vincentian seminary in Chartres, who had been diagnosed with an incurable condition. This recovery was attested by Cardinal de Noailles, the Archbishop of Paris, and Father Bonnet later became Superior General of the Congregation of the Mission. Novena devotions made in Vincent's honour brought forth many more miraculous cures that were confirmed only after the most rigorous scrutiny.

In 1712, Cardinal de Noailles visited the tomb and, when Vincent's body was examined in front of a variety of witnesses, it was found to be incorrupt. Though this phenomenon is not a necessary qualification, it accelerated the cause of his canonisation, and he was beatified in 1729 by Pope Benedict XIII. Miracles attributed to the relics and intercession of the new Beatus continued. A Benedictine nun, for example, recovered from hopeless paralysis when the Bishop of Soissons touched her pain-racked body with a relic. Louisa Sackville, an English lady lodging in Paris was cured of palsy after making a Novena at Vincent's tomb, a recovery confirmed by her landlady the more convincingly because she not share her guest's faith.

Canonisation

Vincent was canonised in 1737 by Pope Clement XII. His house and shrine at Saint-Lazare was sacked during the French Revolution at the end of the century but, happily, his remains were respected and were eventually translated to a new shrine in the Chapel of the Lazarists in the Rue de Sevres, Paris. Originally, Saint Vincent de Paul's feast day was 19th July but, since the revision of the Calendar in 1969, it is now celebrated on 27th September, the anniversary of his death.

Society of Saint Vincent de Paul

Pope Leo XIII, 1878-1903, named Vincent the Patron of all Charitable Societies, and outstanding among them is that which bears his name and is infused with his spirit. Antoine Frederic Ozaman, born in France in 1813, was a distinguished literature scholar, a professor of rhetoric, and an active defender of the Church and her teachings. He was deeply concerned for the poor and, in 1833, founded a religious society of laity who were devoted to helping those whose plight had been made even worse by the impact of industrialisation. He was convinced that the best way of demonstrating Catholic commitment was through works of organised charity and, for that reason chose Saint Vincent de Paul as Patron. As urban poverty and social dislocation grew, the work of the Society became increasingly important and from France it spread to a hundred and twelve countries.

The aims of the Society are to study the teachings of the Church, put them into practice through charitable enterprise and the distribution of alms, to maintain contact with the poor, and to nurture the personal holiness of members who support one another. Weekly meetings include prayers, spiritual reading, instruction, reporting on tasks undertaken, and the allocation of new assignments. Conferences at local, diocesan, national, and international levels are organised as the framework for cooperative endeavour.

Picture of Saint Vincent

A number of existing portraits and statues were inspired by the observations of the Saint's contemporaries. They say that by nature, he was thoughtful and reserved, and some candidly remark that he was less than handsome with a large, balding head and a prominent nose. However, all agree that his face lit with a natural charm and if he was uncompromising about faults, mistakes and errors, he corrected so gently that there was no hurtful offence or discouragement.

His skill and learning as a theologian gave him a natural authority that his humility failed to disguise, and he combined his ardent charity with sound judgement, so that he did not act until he was sure that what he had in mind accorded with God's will. Then, he would let nothing deter him from his purpose. To those who might criticise what they saw as unnecessary delay he would say, "Do not tread on the heels of Providence who is our Guide." He managed to remain erect and active almost to the end of his life, and he never complained about his time as a slave in Tunis even though his constitution had been affected by the arrow-wound, the pirates' savagery, the toil, inadequate nourishment, and lack of sleep in a demanding climate. The highly acclaimed film biography of Vincent, *Monsieur Vincent,* was released in 1947. It was directed by Maurice Cloche, the eminent Jean Anouilh wrote the screenplay and the distinguished actor Pierre Fresney played the Saint. Though it was naturally in French, subtitles and sensitive dubbing ensured its worldwide distribution.

"God our Father, you gave Vincent de Paul the courage and holiness of an apostle for the well-being of the poor and the formation of the clergy. Help us to be zealous in continuing his work" (Opening Prayer, Feast Day).

Writings of Saint Vincent de Paul

Care for the poor

"If you consider the poor in the light of faith, then you will see that they take the place of God the Son who chose to be poor and showed He was to preach the Gospel to the poor with these words, 'He has sent me to preach the good news to the poor.' We should be of the same mind and should imitate what Christ did, caring for the poor, consoling them, helping them, and guiding them."

The love of Jesus

"Christ chose to be born in poverty and took poor men as His disciples. He himself became the servant of the poor and so shared their condition that whatever good or harm was done to the poor, He said He would consider done to Him. Since God loves the poor, He loves the lovers of the poor. When someone loves another, he also loves those who love or serve that other."

Love of our neighbours

"We hope that God will love us on account of the poor, so we visit them, strive to concern ourselves with the weak

and needy, and so share their sufferings that, with the
Apostle Paul, we feel that we have become all things to
all men. We must strive, therefore, to be deeply involved
in the cares and sorrows of our neighbours and pray to
God to inspire us with compassion and pity, filling our
hearts and keeping them full."

Prayer and work

"The service of the poor is to be preferred to all else, and
be performed without delay. If medicine or help has to be
taken to some poor person at a time that had been set aside
for prayer, go and do what has to be done with an easy
mind, offering it up to God as a prayer. Do not feel uneasy
that service of the poor has interrupted prayer, for God is
not neglected if prayers are put aside, or if His work is
interrupted so that another such work may be completed."

Charity first

"When you leave prayer to help the poor, remember that
the work has been done for God. Charity takes
precedence over any rules, everything must be directed
towards it, and what it orders should be carried out. Let
us show our service to the poor with renewed ardour in
our hearts, seeking out any abandoned people above all,
since they are given to us as lords and patrons."

Care for yourself

"Be careful to preserve your health. It is a trick the devil employs to deceive good souls, to incite them to do more than they are able, on order that they may no longer be able to do anything."

Words of wisdom

"We should spend as much time in thanking God for His benefits as we do in asking Him for them."

"The reason why God is so great a lover of humility is because He is a great lover of truth. Now humility is nothing but truth while pride is nothing but lying."

"In this world, things that are naturally to endure for a long time are the slowest in reaching maturity."

"If, in order to succeed in an enterprise, I was obliged to choose between fifty deer commanded by a lion, and fifty lions commanded by a deer, I should consider myself more certain of success with the first group then the second."